Cape Cod Bike Book

A Complete Guide To
The Bike Trails of Cape Cod

Cape Cod Rail Trail, Nickerson Park Trails
Falmouth Woods Hole Trail
National Seashore Trails

William E. Peace

The Cape Cod Bike Book

A Complete Guide To The Bike Trails of Cape Cod

Cape Cod Rail Trail, Nickerson Park Trails, Falmouth Woods Hole Trail,

National Seashore Trails

ISBN-13: 978-1512127478

ISBN-10: 1512127477

Printed in the United States of America

Bicycling on Cape Cod

S omething for everyone on wheels – Cape Cod offers much to bicyclists. It is often said that every town, indeed every village in every town on Cape Cod, has its own character, its own charm. From easy, level paths to challenging and longer routes, from quaint Woods Hole to sometimes foggy Chatham and then to sundrenched Provincetown, there is bicycling on Cape Cod to suit everyone's temperament. There are so many fantastic places to bike on Cape Cod!

Our book is written with that in mind, from an "insider's" view, by a local resident who knows all the ins and outs of Cape Cod, all the back roads, and all the things to see, with the intent of sharing some of these wonderful locations for more to enjoy. All the main bicycle trails are included as well as some custom routes that will get you off-the-beaten path and seeing some gorgeous Cape scenery that others may miss. There are trails or paths in each town of the Cape and QR codes to bring you to custom detailed GPS maps for free use on your phone for every route in every town!

But wherever you bicycle, don't race from place to place. Stop to enjoy the surf, the sand, and the scenery. Explore and enjoy!!

T he service roads along the Cape Cod Canal provide for some of the finest biking and sightseeing that the Cape has to offer. The 8 mile routes run along each side of the Canal, on both north and south sides. Sightseers can view the scenic Bourne and Sagamore Bridges from very unique perspectives unavailable to drivers and can view also the Sandwich Marina, the Canal Electric Plant, the U.S. Coast Guard Station, the Buzzards Bay Railroad Bridge, the Massachusetts Maritime Academy, the National Marine Life Center, Scusset Beach, Scusset Fish Pier and Bourne Scenic Park. The biking is all on the level on wide roads used to service the Canal, and free parking is readily available in several locations.

Parking – Mainland Side of Canal

Sagamore Bridge: On the mainland side of Sagamore Bridge, take the Canal Road, between McDonald's and Dunkin Donuts, and follow the road to the parking area at the Canal.

Scusset Beach: From the mainland side of the Sagamore Bridge, take the signs to Scusset Beach.

Herring River: Go 1 mile west of Sagamore Bridge on Route 6 towards Buzzards Bay; the parking area is on the left, just before the large hill.

Buzzards Bay: Proceed into Buzzards Bay center; just near the railroad station, turn directly toward the Railroad Bridge and the large parking area there.

Bourne Scenic Park: The park is right near the Bourne Bridge on Route 6; there is a charge for very limited picnic ground parking.

Parking – Cape Cod Side of Canal

Freezer Road: From Rt. 6 west on Cape Cod, take Exit 55 to Sagamore. Go east about 1 mile; take Tupper Road on the left and take that to Freezer Road on the left. Parking is at the end of Freezer Road, left of the marina. To reach the Visitor Center parking, turn right at the marina.

Bourne Bridge: From the Bourne Rotary on Route 28 near the Bourne Bridge, take Route 6 toward Hyannis. Then after just 0.1 miles, turn sharply left toward the bridge, then turn right just before the bridge to the parking area.

Google Map QR Code:

About QR Codes:

Use a QR code reader app on your phone or tablet to scan the QR code here. It will immediately take you directly to a custom, detailed Google map showing the bike trail or path's location, driving directions, and exact parking locations. You can then use the trail map on your phone as you bike. More information about QR codes is found on page 99.

Trail Description

At the parking area past and to the left of Sandwich Marina area, there are rest room facilities, a small playground, water fountains, picnic tables, and a splendid place to see the eastern end of the Canal. The Marina itself has been operated by the Town of Sandwich since 1989 and provides boaters with excellent launching facilities and slips, and access to the Cape Cod Bay or the Canal itself. There is always something to see here! There is a small radar tower used in monitoring ships in the Canal, in the shadow of the enormous Canal Electric Plant that you passed on the way in to the area. The electric plant itself has three parts producing 1500 MW of electricy total, and is owned by JeraAmericas based in Houston. The plant is powered by either oil or natural gas; oil and natural gas loading and storage areas are just a short distance to the left.

Around the road to the right of the marina is another large parking area, rest room facilities, a picnic area, and the U.S. Coast Guard Station and Army Corps of Engineers (which has maintained the Canal since 1928) Visitor Center. The Visitor Center is well worth a visit, with many interesting displays explaining how the Canal is used by maritime traffic, including interactive exhibits, films, rangers and volunteers to answer questions, and even a 40 foot patrol boat that you can board!

The Marine Traffic Control exhibit shows how radar and cameras are used to guide ships through the Canal. On the opposite shore of the Canal from this area are the popular Scusset Fish Pier and Scusset Beach.

Notice the PAVE PAWS radar facility on the horizon — this is one of the largest radar facilities in the world, at the Joint Base Cape Cod. This facility is used to detect intercontinental as well as sea-launched missiles. Similar facilities are located in California and in Alaska. The facility is a phased array facility, with three fixed faces monitoring 120 degrees of the horizon each. When first constructed, Cape residents expressed some concerns about the health effects of this facility, as it sends high power radar signals over Cape Cod toward the east; amazingly, it can spot an object the size of a small automobile when it is still over Europe.

The scenery along the Canal itself includes the thousands of boats passing here annually, people lobstering and fishing, many species of seaweeds and animals along the rocks, the gentle terrain, and, of course, the bridges themselves. Be careful, the rocks are steep and slippery, and the Canal current is not forgiving of error. Notice the streams running down the hillsides to the Canal in spots. At one time, two tidal streams followed the course of the Canal, Scusset River easterly into the Bay, and Manamet River flowing into Buzzards Bay. These streams were replaced by the Canal itself, which is 480 - 700 feet wide by 32 feet deep, and was opened to international boating traffic in July 1914. First built as a toll route, the Canal was taken over by the Federal government in 1928; it is now maintained by the Army Corps of Engineers. In 1928, as an improvement effort, the highway bridges were built to replace early drawbridges. With intense traffic over the bridges at times, with more than 125,000 cars per day in the summer season, there is some speculation that a third bridge, or modifications to the current bridges, may be needed in the future to handle the heavy seasonal traffic. Besides the bridges, the Cape

is linked to the mainland by the large electric lines as well. While the three 345 kilovolt and two 115 kilovolt electric lines over the Canal do tarnish the view somewhat, they do provide needed electricity from the New England grid.

Note that the Bourne Bridge is considerably longer than the Sagamore Bridge (2384 feet vs. 1408 feet), having three approach spans on each side compared to Sagamore's one. Both have 135 foot clearances and 661 foot main spans, enough for superstructures of very large ships. The bridges are unquestionably beautiful as well as practical, have won construction and design awards, and serve as symbols of Cape Cod's "identity" and separateness. With their locations exposed to wind and ocean water, they are maintained carefully each year. The vertical lift Railroad Bridge near the Buzzard's Bay end of the

Canal has 1,000 ton counterweights and 50 ton secondary weights. The 544 foot moving section, lifted in 2-3 minutes by 200 horsepower electric motors, weighs 2,200 tons. Trains from Hyannis travel through to Boston. The railroad is also used by some Cape Cod communities year round to transport waste to a waste-to-energy plant in Wareham.

Bicyclists on the mainland can enjoy a rest or swim at the Scusset Beach area, a splendid dune-backed white sand beach, with views to Cape Cod and Cape Cod Bay. At the Railroad Bridge in Buzzards Bay, those looking for more biking can proceed through the parking lot, turn left on Main Street, then left onto Academy Drive. It is about a 1 mile round trip to the Massachusetts Maritime Academy. Here you can see the wind turbine closeup, and may see the training vessel or other ships harbored here. The views into Buzzards Bay and the west end of the Canal, and the boating traffic here, are stunning. At the Railroad Bridge is also the Buzzard's Bay Train Station, the beautiful Buzzard's Bay Park and Playground, a large parking area, and the National Marine Life Center. Here, sea turtles and seals, dolphins, porpoises and small whales are rehabilitated and released back to the wild. A visitor center and gift store is open to the public and provides a great resting spot from the biking.

Falmouth Shining Sea Trail

T his trail, first dedicated in 1975, and named in honor of Kathryn Lee Bates, the author of "America the Beautiful", extends 10.7 miles from Woods Hole to County Road in North Falmouth. The trail passes gorgeous ocean views of Vineyard Sound on the south and Buzzards Bay on the west. Kathryn was born in Falmouth in 1859 and had lived in the family home on Main Street until 1871, just a few blocks to the east of the trail, at the Falmouth Village Green.

Parking

Locust Street: Take Route 28 to Falmouth. At the west end of town, follow signs toward Woods Hole, onto Locust St. About 1/4 mile down Locust Street is Mill Road, on the left. A short distance farther on Locust Street, on the right, is a small lot for parking.

Depot Avenue: Additional parking is just north on Depot Avenue, just past the newspaper offices. Parking is difficult at best in Woods Hole itself during the summer.

County Road: At the north end of the trail, a large parking area is also available at County Road in North Falmouth.

Old Dock Road: During non-boating seasons, parking is also available at Old Dock Road, a short distance just off Palmer Avenue.

Trail Description — Depot Street to Woods Hole

The Falmouth Shining Sea Trail follows the Old Colony Railroad (later the New Haven Railroad and then the Penn Central Railroad) grade between Woods Hole and North Falmouth. For nearly 100 years until 1965, trains had run between New York City and Woods Hole. For the most part, the south trail is very straight and quite level, making a fine trail for beginners.

As you start out biking south from Depot Street and cross Locust Street, notice the large locusts and maples along the path; they make for an especially pleasant ride. Soon there is a view of Salt Pond to the left of the trail and a beautiful marsh area to the right. Listen for the many birds, and look for marsh plants and the fine Atlantic white cedars. Can you catch a glimpse of the Atlantic on the horizon?

Continuing on this sunny, open trail, at the paved road (Elm Road), a view to Quisset Beach (named after the Quisset

Native Americans) is seen. This is a fine beach for swimming, with jetties to visit and typical beach plants to observe – beachgrass, Dusty Miller, seaside goldenrod, and beach pea. This is a fragile but important protective ecosystem; be careful not to harm the plants in this area. From the beach, there are also distant views of Nobska Light to the right. Across Elm Road, the bike path continues past Oyster Pond on the right, with views through the marsh grass to Quisset on the hill. Oyster Pond, like Salt Pond, is a kettle pond, formed tens of thousands of years ago by the glacier. At that time, occasional large blocks of ice were left behind, partially buried and surrounded by soil. As they melted, they left large indentations filled with water. Crossing Surf Drive at the beach, the trail continues right along the ocean's edge, along the beach; this is the only Cape bike trail to do so. Here there are close views of Martha's Vineyard on your left as you pass across the dunes at the ocean's edge.

Crossing the Trunk River Herring run, the path provides more views of Nobska to the left and Quisset to the right. Soon the path begins a gradual turn away from the ocean and continues quite level through oak woods, then pitch pine woods, past many nice homes, some with exquisite landscaping, and with views to the left of Martha's Vineyard Sound. Passing several rock-strewn hillsides, reminders of the glacier's work here thousands of years ago, the trail soon enters a parking lot for the Oceanographic Institute, passing through it, then under a large bridge (Church Street), and to the very edge of Little Harbor in Woods Hole.

Passing under another bridge, the trail brings you to the parking area for the Steamship Authority, which provides Nantucket and Martha's Vineyard ferries. Use caution biking in this area due to the heavy traffic. Just to the right and then to the left is Water Street, with its quaint atmosphere, harbor views, restaurants, and more. Woods Hole is the scientific center of the Cape, with the Oceanographic Institute, the Marine Fisheries and their public aquaria, great for kids, and the Marine Biology Labs. In the 1800's this was an important port for the whaling industry.

A side route to Nobska Lighthouse proceeds along the right side of the state highway, up the hill from the Steamship Authority lot, back toward Boston. Take the first right, Church Street, down past the church to Nobksa Pond, Nobska beach, and Nobska lighthouse. "Nobska" is the Wampanoag Native

American term for "rocky point", which you can see is an apt name for this area. The lighthouse is a great place to see, with views over the Vineyard Sound. This is a well-travelled but dangerous route, so use extreme caution. Be certain to return by the same route, as the rest of the road is even more twisting and narrow. However, the extraordinary views and the rocky shore make this route very inviting.

Trail Description – Depot Street to North Falmouth

Completed in 2009, the trail north from Depot Street brings you along the eastern edge of the hills formed by the glacier (Buzzards Bay moraine) nearly 25,000 years ago. Beebe Woods, a large woodland area on this moraine, is great for a quiet hike; it is off the trail, just up Depot Street to Highfield Drive. As you pass north of Highfield Drive, you will be passing Falmouth Academy on the left and the Steamship Authority parking areas on the right. Falmouth Hospital is just to the left just before Ter Heun Drive. As you travel north from Ter Heun Drive, you will soon head more toward the west, then leave the moraine area and travel along the Buzzard's Bay shore. As you travel through this area of the moraine, you will notice the occasional granite rocks near the trail. These are called glacial erratics – they are boulders deposited by the conveyer-like motions of the glacier and originated from north in Massachusetts and New Hampshire.

Buzzards Bay itself is an important marine environment, supporting in particular large bluefish and striped bass populations. The name "Buzzard" actually was an error by the early

 settlers – the bird that they were observing was actually the osprey; nearly extinct in the 1960's, the osprey is now making a strong comeback

and can be seen nesting on many high platforms in the area. As you travel in this area north to County Road in North Falmouth, you will bike past many fine views first of Little Sippewisset Marsh, then the Saconesset Hills, then the Great Sippewisset marshes and finally Snug Harbor and West Falmouth Harbor. This is truly the beautiful America that Katharine Lee Bates had written about. The marshes themselves are not just beautiful, but very important ecosystems that trap huge amounts of the sun's energy and pass it through the food chains to many marine species. Because of their location near Woods Hole, these marshes have been extensively studied by ecologists and biologists.

Past the Great Marsh, Chapaquoit Road will bring you to the left to Chapaquoit Beach, a great beach spot to relax before continuing on. A little farther north, Old Dock Road will bring you to the fantastic views at the harbor area. Back on the main trail you will soon pass several cranberry bogs, with Wing Pond to the left. Cranberries are an important crop here on Cape Cod, with Massachusetts providing nearly 25% of the nation's cranberries. The berries thrive in moist, acidic conditions that can be found in this area. This particular bog area has been in use since the 1860's. Several restaurants, banks, and other businesses are available as the trail continues north close to Route 28A and then to North Falmouth at County Road.

Google Map QR Code:

Osterville / Marstons Mill / Mashpee

T his scenic route begins in Osterville Center and takes you to several views of North Bay and West Bay near Osterville, to Osterville Center, and the famous estates of the Osterville area. The full trip is 5 miles, but there are many rest spots. Few facilities are available, though.

Parking

Osterville Center: Park in the municipal parking lot behind the stores in Osterville.

Trail Description – Osterville / Marstons Mill

It was in Marstons Mill that in 1689 that Benjamin Marston had built the first "fulling mill" in the U.S.. It was used to finish rough cloth. The actual mill was blown down in a storm in 1930, but the old dam is still left at Mill Pond and Mills River at the intersection of Route 149 and 28. A herring run and ladder is found here now, making this a very popular springtime spot. There is a small parking place just across from Mill Pond. It is a nice spot to stop before or after your bike ride in this area.

From the municipal parking lot at Osterville Center, turn left onto Main Street and then left onto Bay Street. This brings you, by downhill coasting for much of the way, past many finely landscaped properties to a dead-end water access with exceptional views of North Bay. Saint Mary's Island is to the far right, and Baxter Neck is across the Bay to the right. Straight across the water is Point Isabella, and to the far left is the bridge to Little Island and Osterville Grand Island, Little Island being to the left. This is a wonderful spot to view boating on North Bay and to enjoy the sunshine; it really is a goal in itself.

Returning via Bay Street, turn right at the intersection onto Parker Road, then turn right again onto West Bay Road. Continue straight ahead past the golf course, and at the end of West Bay Road, you will reach Crosby Boat Yard, with fine views of the commercial boating enterprise and also a snack bar and yacht shop. Turning off West Bay Road onto Bridge Street will take you to a larger town landing, right at the bend of the road, with expansive views. Here there is a small marsh and a view to West Bay, with Wianno straight across the water. Osterville Grand Island is to the right with the large homes visible along the shore.

Back onto Bridge Street, turn left and then bike over the metal bridge and coast gently down onto Little Island. This bridge was first built in the 1890's, as a way to link the islands to the mainland. Bridge Street follows the causeway that was built between the islands at that time. As you travel over the causeway, you will finally reach a salt marsh area on both sides of the road, with views of West Bay to the left and North Bay to the right. Before the bridge and causeway were built, farmers would graze their animals on Great Island, but could only get access by taking animals along Dead Neck and then across to the island at low tide. Because of private roads on Osterville Grand Island, you must turn back at the windmill, retracing your path onto West Bay Road. Here, take your first right, Eel

River Road, where you will find pleasant coasting, and some level biking, too. Proceed through the residential area. At the end of Eel River Road, turn right onto Seaview Avenue to pass views of Eel River to the right, then uphill and level to the end of Seaview Avenue where you can see Dead Neck to the left, with Osterville Grand Island to the right, West Bay also to the right, and the channel to the ocean and the light to the left.

There are three bays in the Osterville area, West Bay that we see here, North Bay that we had seen from Bay Road, and Cotuit Bay on the other side of Osterville Grand Island. Dead Neck Island was originally connected to the mainland. Accessing West Bay by boat required entering Cotuit Bay, then navigating up Santuit River along the north shore of Dead Neck Island. A cut was made in 1901 to allow for direct access to West Bay from the ocean. This is the same channel with jetties along the sides that you can see from Seaview Avenue, Unfortunately, jetties do alter the natural flow of sand in the area, in this case, causing some erosion on Dead Neck. Dredging of the channels is periodically used to replenish sand on Dead Neck itself.

Returning to Eel River Road, continue on Sea View Avenue past Eel River Road for an easy ride down to West Street on the left. As you ride along Sea View Avenue, Nantucket Sound is to the right and Nantucket Island is about 28 miles across the Sound. At West Street, turn left, going past the Wianno Golf Club on the left, and then follow West Street and Crystal Lake Road to its end at Wianno Avenue. Then turn left at Wianno Avenue to head back into Osterville Center. If you are looking for more distance on your ride, you can continue past the Center and onto a pleasant ride on South County Road. After passing through the Center, keep to the right at the intersection to travel onto South County Road.

Google Map QR Code:

Mashpee Bike Trail

You can park for this trail at 524 Route 130 at the Mashpee Heritage Park. At Heritage Park itself, there is excellent parking and also a playground as well as basketball courts, softball, baseball and other athletic fields. This pleasant, easy ride runs south about 3 miles along Route 130, past the Mashpee Wampanoag Museum, a beach on Mashpee Pond (to reach the pond, go left on Lake Avenue) and a fine herring run observation area at Mashpee River. The trail then passes through residential areas and ends at Meadow Haven Road, near Route 28. North from the Heritage Park, you can also travel about 1 mile to Pickeral Cove Road.

Google Map QR Code:

Lewis Bay, Hyannisport

T his route, along the docks and waterfront park in Hyannis, also travels past some beautiful beaches, the Kennedy Memorial, and ends at the Kennedy Compound area in Hyannisport. The route is 8 miles round trip, but there are many stops. Most is on level ground. Traffic in this area is heavy, though, so be especially careful.

Parking

Main Street, Hyannis: Take Route 28 or Route 132 to the Airport Rotary. Take Barnstable Road (south from the rotary) and follow this to the lights on Main Street in Hyannis, turning right there. Just after the Post Office on the left and before the Library, there is a narrow entryway to public parking.

North Street: There is additional parking on North Street, behind the stores on the other side of Main Street. Some parking is also at Hyannis Harbor, Kalmus Park Beach, Veterans Park, and Keyes Memorial Beach.

Trail Description

Leaving the rear of the parking lot on Main Street, first walk across South Street using particular caution, as the traffic is heavy and fast here. Proceeding to your left, you will pass the former National Armory on the right; President John Kennedy had given his nomination acceptance speech here. On the left is the Barnstable Town Hall. The Town Hall, one of the first brick structures on Cape Cod, was originally the Hyannis Normal School for Teachers, and later became Cape Cod Community College until the College moved to its current location on Route 132.

After 0.1 mile, turn right onto Old Colony Road, and proceed 0.2 miles to a left turn onto Bay Street. Follow this short street to Ocean Street, where there are wonderful views of Hyannis Inner Harbor at the Park. Here there is a pedestrian walkway along the docks, fascinating fishing activity to watch daily, benches, restrooms, and several seafood restaurants. In the summer, there are Artists Shanties at the Park here, with arts of all different types on display and for sale. Hyannis Har-

bor has been an important commercial harbor for hundreds of years, and continues its importance in fishing, commuting, and sightseeing still. This is a place with some real Cape Cod flavor.

Continue on Ocean Street past the restaurant on the left and take your first left (Channel Point Road), then turn right from here onto Daisy Bluff. From here, keep to the left with the ocean to your left as you proceed onto Bay Shore Road. Follow this for some distance. 0.1 mile onto Bay Shore there is a fine town boat landing with water access. Oftentimes there are ducks to see here, and there is a sweeping view of Lewis Bay, its boats and docks, with West Yarmouth on the horizon.

Continue on Bay Shore, keeping close to the shore itself until you reach the dead end and stop signs, and turn right onto Harbor Bluff. Here, you will soon pass another town way to the water with gorgeous views of the Bay and Great Island directly across the water and the dunes of Kalmus Park Beach to the right. Continue straight to another dead end sign and bear right to come to Ocean Street, turning left. It is 0.1 mile to the Kennedy Memorial and a town park to the right of the fence. At the meticulously-maintained Kennedy Memorial, there are granite benches, a stunning view, and a memorial plaque and fountain in honor of President Kennedy. You really should not just bike by this area, it is well worth the stop. Rest facilities, swimming, parking, swings, picnic and cookout areas are also available at the Veterans Memorial Park just to the right of the Kennedy Memorial. There is also a Korean War Memorial to see, found between the Kennedy Memorial and the picnic area.

Leaving the Memorial area and turning left, proceed on Ocean Street to beautiful Kalmus Park Beach where swimming, snack bar, facilities, and parking are available. Then go straight out of the beach parking area, finally turning right onto Estey Avenue and then left on Gosnold and left at its end onto Sea Street. From there, it is a short distance to Keyes Memorial (Sea Street) Beach, a popular beach with picnic area, bath

house, snacks, and parking. In the distance, the Kennedy Compound is past the breakwater to the right. Continue around the curve on Ocean Avenue, past the large marsh area on the right (Stewart's Creek) where you may see swans or ducks.

You can continue on these roads, keeping to the left close to the ocean until you reach the intersection of Scudder Avenue and Irving Avenue. As you travel on Irving Avenue, you will pass one of the Kennedy homes on the left, secluded behind the very high hedges. Unfortunately, this is as close as you can get to the Compound; the best way to see the Compound is from the water – there are tours that leave from Hyannis Harbor that provide a great view of the Kennedy Compound. To get back to your parking area, you can return via the same path or can take a shorter route up Scudder Avenue to South Street or Main Street, where you can enjoy the many restaurants and businesses of Hyannis.

Trail Description – Old Stage Bikepath

This path begins at the Route 6 service road and Route 149. There is no parking available, however. The path proceeds over rolling terrain through pine/oak woods and a residential area to Race Lane. Here it continues to the left along Old Stage Road to Route 28 and then proceeds along Route 28, 2 miles east to Bearse's Way. Sections of the trail are dangerous, as not all is off-road, and some of it is close to very fast highways.

Google Map QR Code:

Parking

Rail Trail, Station Avenue: There is a large parking for the Rail Trail on Station Avenue in South Yarmouth, just south of Exit 75, Route 6, near the pedestrian bridge.

Rail Trail, Homer Park: Parking at Homer Park is available from Rt. 6, Exit 75. Take Union Street/Station Avenue south from Route 6 0.7 miles to the second set of lights; turn right on Old Townhouse Road. The Park is 0.6 miles on the right.

Bayberry Hills: A small parking lot is found just after West Yarmouth Road on the left side of Old Townhouse Road, at the entrance to the Bayberry Hills Golf Course.

Trail Description — Rail Trail in Yarmouth

For many years, the Cape Cod Rail Trail had started in South Dennis. With new construction from Yarmouth to Dennis completed in 2018, the Rail Trail now begins at Homer Park in South Yarmouth. The trail passes along the left edge of the playing fields to the back of the park and then east behind the industrial area, soon reaching the new pedestrian bridge crossing Station Avenue; here several restaurants and grocery and convenience stores are found.

Continuing east, the trail passes through pitch pine woods and several residential neighborhoods. About 1.1 miles past Station Avenue, at Dupont Avenue, you can take Dupont itself to the right another half mile to the Flax Pond Recreation area; here there are playgrounds, play areas, and a freshwater swimming area with bath houses and restrooms in season.

From Dupont Avenue, the trail trail continues east through pitch pine woods, parallel to White's Path, with a heavily used business area about 200 feet to the left of the trail. The path soon reaches North Main Street. At North Main Street, use caution, this is a very busy intersection.

A new bridge, the George Allaire Bridge, now replaces the old railroad bridge over Bass River. The views of Bass River here are gorgeous! Just before the bridge, the trail parallels the highway just a hundred feet or so away from Route 6 itself, on a slight bluff looking down on the roadway; residential areas are on the right of the trail. Route 6 extends all the way from Provincetown to Bishop, California. While there are large seasonal variations in traffic flow here, and more than 50,000 vehicles per day in the summer passing here, the highway is a vital transportation route for Cape Cod year round.

Trail Description — Yarmouth Bike Path

Leaving from the parking place at Homer Park on Old Townhouse Road, starting just behind the facilities building, is the Yarmouth Bike Path that travels west, to the left, just over 2 miles through gently rolling terrain to Higgins Crowell Road in

West Yarmouth, where the bike trail currently ends. Plans exist to extend the trail eventually to Willow Street and then into conservation lands west of Willow Street. From Homer Park, the trail first follows along Old Town House Road, with views of the Bayberry Hills golf course to the right. After crossing West Yarmouth Road and the entranceway to the golf course (use caution here due to the heavy traffic), the trail heads south along the golf course boundary, through the pleasant pitch pine woods, with views of the golf course to the right, then heads west to reach Higgins Crowell Road.

Google Map QR Code:

T he Dennis North-South Trail runs from historic South Dennis to the beautiful north side and Scargo Hill Tower and Hokum Rock. The Cape Rail Trail itself begins in Yarmouth, passes through South Dennis, and continues east into Harwich. Another route south from South Dennis brings you to picturesque West Dennis and West Dennis Beach. The Setucket/Old Chatham/134 trail takes you through Dennis from the Johnny Kelly Recreation area, past the Town Hall area, and through rolling woodland along Setucket and Old Chatham Roads.

Parking

Rail Trail, Main Street: Large parking is at 495 Main Streeet, South Dennis, 0.5 miles south of Route 6 on Main Street, at the new Rail Trail parking location.

Rail Trail, Route 134: Additional parking is near the pedestrian bridge on Route 134. From Route 6 take Route 134 south past the mall. Rail Trail parking is about 0.2 mile farther south on the left.

North-South and Setucket Trails – Johnny Kelley Recreation area: From Route 134, go north past the Mall area and turn left on Bob Crowell Road, just before the Police Station. Just before the end of Crowell Road, turn left into the parking area for the Kelley Recreation area. An additional parking area is just around the corner to the left, on Old Bass River Road. Follow Old Bass River Road about 1 mile south for parking at the old Town Hall area on Main Street

South and West Dennis Trail: Park either at the Rail Trail parking at 495 Main Street, South Dennis, at the Ezra Baker School on Route 28 in West Dennis, or at West Dennis Beach.

Trail Description — Rail Trail, Bass River to Rt. 134

At Bass River, you can see the new pedestrian bridge built in 2018. Due to its narrow width, the old railroad bridge here, built originally in 1816, had restricted water flow to upper parts of the River; it was removed in 2010. The new bridge allows for a much wider flow of the river below and for pedestrian and bicycle crossing. There are fine views here of Bass River and Kelley's Bay, both to the north, past Route 6, and to the south as well. Looking south, the Nobscusset Conservation Lands are to the left of the river and the Blue Rock residential area in Yarmouth is to the right. After the trail passes over Bass River, it continues east, with an old cranberry bog visible briefly on the right.

About 0.3 miles east of Bass River is a path to the right that brings you to walking trails on the Nobscusset Conservation area, often called the "Indian Lands". Before the area was settled in the 1600's, the Native American Nobscusset tribe had spent its winters along Bass River in this area, protected from the heavy storms that would hit the north side of Dennis. During summers, they would live and farm north of Route 6A near the beaches there. The Conservation area is a wonderful walk and brings you to expansive views of Bass River and is well worth a stop. Bicycling is not allowed in the Conservation area itself. The Rail Trail itself continues to the east through pitch pine woods, with the power lines to the right.

At Main Street in South Dennis, use caution crossing this very busy street. An interesting Ancient cemetery, well worth exploring, is found here on the right, just behind the former location of the Dennis Town Hall. Here many members of the Baker, Nickerson, Crowell, and Berry families are buried. The oldest slate stone here is dated 1711 and the person buried there had died at just 19 years of age. Across Main Street, the rail trail follows the railroad grade east along the property of a coal/oil company and a lumber yard; in recent decades this was one of the last stops on the railroad which brought lumber to the lumber yard and coal to the coal/oil company, but that use was discontinued when trains no longer travelled past Yarmouth. Several factors led to the decline of the use of the railroad in this area, but the building of the mid-Cape highway in the 1950's made highway transport to the mid-Cape much more efficient, and this ultimately led to the end of the use of the railway in this area in the 1960's. Once across the pedestrian bridge over Route 134, the trail continues east toward Harwich and Chatham.

Trail Description — Rail Trail East from Route 134

This section of the trail begins at the Rail Trail parking lot on Route 134 and heads east through pitch pine and oak woods on a very level easy-to-bike path to Depot Street in Dennis Port. South Dennis had been the western-most point of the trail since the 1980's, but in 2018, construction extended the trail toward Barnstable, through Yarmouth. The Rail Trail follows the railway that had been originally built in the mid 1800's by the Old Colony Railroad, which ran trains to Provincetown from Boston and New York.

As you start east from Route 134, notice the Cape Cod Regional Transit Authority Northwind 100 wind turbine on the left, which generates more than 180,000 kWh per year. The Transit Authority itself runs year-round bus service throughout the Cape, as well as door-to-door rides and medical rides to Boston. At Gages Way, the first crossing, you can follow the sidewalk to the left 0.2 miles to see a very large 6 megawatt solar installation, one of the largest in the state. It provides electricity to the municipal buildings as well as to the local school district. At Great Western Road, use caution in crossing – it is best to walk across most intersections on the Rail Trail. At Depot Street, following Depot Street to the right takes you to the many shops of famous Dennis Port. There are several restaurants in the area, as well as shops of many kinds, from antiques to art galleries to groceries and gifts.

Trail Description — North / South Trail

For this trail, you can park at the Rail Trail parking at 495 Main Street, South Dennis, or at Johnny Kelley Park. To reach the path, turn left from the Main Street lot to head north and then cross over Route 6. Just past Route 6, the off-road bike path begins and then passes the Johnny Kelley area. While in spots this path is very close to Bass River Road's fast traffic, it does traverse some very pleasant scenery of the Mid-Cape area and is certainly an enjoyable ride. The trail here is passing from the very level area south of Route 6, to a higher and hillier area to the north. The hilly area to the north of Route 6 here, called a moraine, was formed nearly 25,000 years ago by the Wisconsin glacier which stalled at the time, and deposited the hills in a conveyer-belt motion. The level area to the south of Route 6 was formed by sand and gravel washing off the glacier for thousands of years. Bass River itself was carved by large flows of water from the glacier.

As the path passes Hokum Rock Road, use particular caution. There is a steep hill down from Hokum Road toward Scargo Hill Road. Cars coming from Scargo Road on the right have poor visibility of bicyclists and may not expect them. Children especially may have difficulty anticipating and stopping at this location. The North-South path itself ends in Dennis Village at the foot of the hill.

From here, side trips to Corporation Beach, Chapin Beach, or Dennis Village would be very worthwhile. At Corporation Beach, fishing and commercial activities thrived in the 1800's until a storm in 1898. At Chapin, Aquaculture Research Corporation, which grows seed clams, can be seen. Just a half mile up Scargo Road from the bike trail is the famous Scargo Tower with its panoramic view of much of Cape Cod. The le-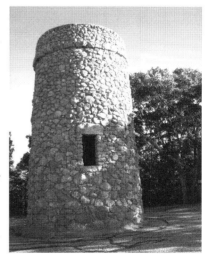gend about Scargo Lake is that it was dug by the Nobscusset Indians for their Princess Scargo's pet fish — the hill formed as the dirt was dug out and the lake filled with her tears because the fish had died. Actually, the Wisconsin glacier formed both the lake and the hills thousands of years ago. 0.7 mile up Hokum Road, on the right of Hokum Rock Road, you will find the famous cave-like Hokum Rock. Supposedly a native lived in the cave here and called out "Ho kum?" whenever anyone came near, but it is a great place to explore and imagine what might have been.

Trail Description — South and West Dennis

Begin your biking on this path at the Rail Trail Parking area on Main Street in South Dennis. During the 1800's, a train depot for South Dennis had existed just north of the parking area. The "Ancient Cemetery" near the parking area holds some of the oldest gravesites in the town, and is fascinating to explore. To the north of the parking area there is a pathway to the left to the Nobscusset Conservation area, formerly called the "Indian Lands", where native Americans here had wintered along the shores of Bass River; the area is a great short hike with expansive views of the River. From the old Town Hall parking area on Main Street, turn right, first passing a charming area of classic New England homes.

The South Dennis Historic District itself contains homes that are carefully restored and maintained in true historic character and create, with a few exceptions, an authentic 19th century village. Continue straight on Main Street, through the village, using caution at the busy "Four Corners" intersections.

At Cove Road, turn right to travel the easy half mile to the pleasant and extensive views of Grand Cove at the town access at the end of the road. Until the early 1900's, here there had been a bridge directly across to Cove Road in West Dennis, but the bridge was ruined by ice at that time, and never replaced. Back on the bike route, Main Street soon curves and winds considerably, so be cautious. Part way into a very sharp curve to the right is Trotting Park Road (to the left). Trotting Park will bring you to the Baker School parking. Here, cross Route 28 cautiously. Trotting Park was for many years the site of a half mile horse racing track but is now a quiet residential area. Continue on Trotting Park to the stop sign, then turn right onto Lower County Road, and then after another half mile, turn left at the sign to the beach.

West Dennis Beach is a full facility beach with many things to see. It is a wonderful place for children and adults alike, with a wide sandy swimming area and beautiful views all year round. The beach itself is nearly a mile in length. If you are here at the right time, you could enjoy fishing, windsailing, and might see some interesting wildlife from foxes to coyotes (early in the morning), to snowy owls, sand pipers and piping plovers, and of course, the many herring gulls.

Trail Description – Setucket/Old Chatham/134 Trail

For access to this trail, you can park at Johnny Kelley Recreation area or at the Town Municipal lot at the intersection of Route 134 and Bob Crowell Road. The trail begins just north of the Town Buildings, on Route 134, and travels on a bike path along the left side of Route 134, past several businesses including grocery and restaurant locations. The path extends 1.4 miles from Bob Crowell Road to Setucket Road, where you can turn left and travel through rolling pitch-pine woods about 3 miles to Route 6A in Yarmouth. 0.4 miles up Setucket Road is the Bell Conservation area with nice walking trails, a picnic area, and nice views of Grassy Pond. 1.6 miles from Route 134 on Setucket is the Flax Pond Conservation area with hiking trails and water views of Flax Pond. At Old Bass River Road, 0.6 miles from Route 134, you can turn south on the North-South bike trail, and this will bring you to Old Chatham Road, where you can turn left to go back to Route 134 at the Wixon School, or you can stay on the North-South trail to reach the Johnny Kelley Recreation area again.

Google Map QR Code:

T his section of the Rail Trail continues east from Dennis into Harwich and then turns north toward Pleasant Lake. Many fine cranberry bogs, marshes, and Cape woodlands can be seen along this easy-to-bike section. It is a short 4 miles from Depot Street in Dennis Port to Pleasant Lake in Harwich. A side spur takes you past beautiful Harwich Center.

Parking

Headwaters Drive: Take Route 6 to Route 124 north at Exit 82. Turn left on Headwaters Drive. Parking is 0.2 miles on the left, after the cranberry bogs

Hinkley's Pond: There is a very small parking for 5-6 cars across Route 124 from the Pleasant Lake store (no parking at the store!!)

Brooks Park: Take Oak Street, the first left off Main Street, which is left off of Route 124 south from Route 6.

Trail Description — Rail Trail in Harwich

The Cape Cod Rail Trail continues east from Depot Street in Dennis Port (see Rail Trail in Dennis), soon reaching Bells Neck Road. This dirt road, followed to the right, brings you to Harwich Conservation Land and a quiet spot with picturesque views of West Reservoir on the right and East Reservoir on the left. These beautiful ponds drain into the Herring River which flows from here to the ocean just south of Lower County Road. The road itself, followed to the left after the reservoir, comes to small pedestrian bridge over the Herring River. Enjoy the marsh grasses in the breeze, the sounds of the wind and the gulls, and the pleasant marsh smell.

Continuing on the main rail trail, we soon see a small cranberry bog on the left and then cross Great Western Road. Be cautious here due to the heavy traffic, and cross on foot.

Soon you will pass several larger bogs, with good views in season of this busy and important Cape Cod industry. Harwich is one of the largest producers of cranberries on the Cape. Indeed, in the 1800's, schools would recess during picking season. Now mechanical harvesters speed the process and increase efficiency. Most students these days would never have heard of a cranberry recess.

At Lothrop Road, you could take a side route to Harwichport and the beaches and harbors to the south, a worthwhile detour. From Lothrop Road, the main trail passes first an interesting marsh area and then an impenetrable "Cape Cod briar patch". An oil truck spill at Great Western and Lothrop had leaked into this area several years ago. Monitoring wells can still be seen in the area. Stop just past here to look for the lichens on the trees — you should be able to see several kinds, and also the large Polytrichum moss on the ground. Continue past the stand of black locusts with their curiously wrinkled bark and then a small stream that drains into the Herring River.

Past the business area on the left (once a lumber yard) is an interesting wetland on the right, with many birds to see and hear. Here, the main trail turns left at the rotary. A spur (see below) heads to the right toward Chatham. On the main trial, notice that the direction changes here more directly toward the north; note also the gradual ascent as the trail slowly climbs the glacial deposit (moraine). These hills were deposited gradually by the actions of the Wisconsin glacier over thousands of years time.

Passing by a cranberry bog on the left and then through typical Cape pine/oak woods, you soon reach a small stand of several types of cedar trees and arrive at Queen Anne Road. Continue straight ahead here, crossing the highway on the bicycle trail bridge. Do stop to watch the traffic here! Cars are an unfortunate priority on Cape Cod, but it is nice to know that the Rail Trail can free us from such travel at times. Continue on the trail past the parking area and behind the large cranberry bogs and Hinkley's Pond to arrive at Pleasant Lake area.

Old Colony Rail Trail – Harwich to Chatham

Taking the right turn at the rotary mentioned above brings you on a pleasant 5 mile ride through Harwich, to Chatham center; be careful where this trail crosses Route 39 and several other roads. Turning off the trail to the right just after the cemetery will bring you directly to Harwich Center with its art galleries, library, groceries, hardware, gasoline station, and Post Office. Past Route 39, the trail continues through Harwich Conservation Lands to the Chatham line. See page 90 for more detail on the Harwich to Chatham trail.

Google Map QR Code:

T his section of the Rail Trail passes north and east through Brewster to Orleans. Gorgeous lake views, especially in the Pleasant Lake area, rolling woodlands, access to Brewster and East Brewster villages, and several ice cream shops make this section of the trail a delight.

Parking

Headwaters Drive: Take Route 6 to Route 124 north at Exit 82. Turn left on Headwaters Drive. Parking is 0.2 miles on the left, after the cranberry bogs

Hinkley's Pond: There is a very small parking for 5-6 cars across Route 124 from the Pleasant Lake store (no parking at the store!!)

Route 137: There is a large parking lot on Long Pond Road

(Route 137), near the intersection with Underpass Road

Underpass Road: There is parking at the Eddy Elementary School and an additional small parking area right on Underpass Road about 0.2 miles from Route 137 on Underpass Road, accessed from the entranceway to the school

Route 124: You will find this parking about 0.1 mile north of Seymour Pond, on the right side of Route 124

Nickerson State Park: There is a large parking area to the right of the entrance building. Another lot is about 0.1 miles west on Route 6A, on the same side of the road as the Park entrance

Trail Description — Rail Trail in Brewster

After a short ride through the woods past the Pleasant Lake Store and area, the trail comes out into the open, passing Long Pond on the right with Route 124 on the left. This is a delightful, level ride with splendid views of this large pond. Covering 716 acres with depths up to 66 feet, Long Pond is the largest freshwater pond on Cape Cod. Unfortunately, there is no public access to the water along most parts of the trail, but the view is still a gorgeous one. The ponds in this area are "kettle ponds", formed by chunks of ice that were buried in glacial material some 25,000 years ago. Seymour Pond, 183 acres in size and about 33 feet at the deepest, is on your left after you pass Long Pond, and is a particularly good example of a kettle pond. Unfortunately, both of these ponds have suffered in recent years from excessive nutrient load which contributes some to algae growth. Use caution in crossing busy Route 124, being sure to heed the signs that you should walk, rather than ride, across roadways.

After the trail leaves the Route 124 area, it trends gently

upward to Route 137 first through Brewster State Forest and then along the Sheep Pond Woodlands. Following Route 137 itself one mile to the left brings you to Brewster Center. Just after Route 137 you will pass the access to the Eddy Elementary School. There is a small playground behind the elementary

school on the left. At Underpass Road, cold drinks and a sandwich shop on the right beckon here to those who want a real treat. The trail continues on fairly level terrain. Thad Ellis Road to the left brings you in 0.1 miles to a convenience store and small restaurant area. At Ober Road, a short walk to the left brings you to a hot dog, hamburger, fried clams, soft serve restaurant right on 6A; this restaurant has been in business here since the 1940's and is definitely worth a stop! Across Route 6A from here, a short 0.5 mile trip down Linnell Landing Road brings you to a gorgeous beach with nice views, sandy beach, tidal flats, a spacious observation platform overlooking Cape Cod Bay ... it is a goal in itself. The Rail Trail then continues to Nickerson State Park, then through the underpass to the Orleans section of the Rail Trail.

Nickerson State Park Trails

Named for Roland Nickerson who worked on railroads in the West, this several thousand acre park was donated to the

state in the 1930's, creating a bit of "wildness forever" on Cape Cod. Here there is free picnicking near the restrooms and freshwater swimming at Flax Pond. On the Park Road trail,

there is a store offering ice creams, snacks, sodas, and other supplies. In the spring, campsites are fairly easy to obtain, but in the summer ask for procedures at the gate.

Park Road Trail – This follows the Park Road bringing you into the center of the Park. Terrain is rolling and the total distance is 3 miles, one way. The access to the trail is behind the main buildings from the bicycle parking area. Past fine woods with pitch pines, the trail also provides views of white pines, spruces, and views of several ponds. The Park store is along this route.

Ober Trail – Accessed from the Park Road Trail, this is a fine trail that extends to the westernmost areas of the Park. Passing the edge of a small pond on the left, the trail also passes the old Crosby gravesite, some stately white pines which were once common on Cape, then some spruces, and finally past views of a fascinating cedar swamp on the left. The trail is about 1.4 miles in length.

Middle Trail – This trail is a pleasant, easy 0.3 mile ride through an oak and pitch pines woodland, ending at the Park Road near the store.

Cedar Trail – A short, easy ride along the entire length of the Old Cedar Swamp, ending near the store on the Park Road

Ruth Pond and Overlook Trails – A picturesque though difficult trail in places, through stands of red pines and along the hills overlooking Ruth Pond, a quiet and refreshing spot in itself.

Nook Park Road Trail – This trail follows the Nook Park Road deep into the park, ending in the southeast area of the park. The trail is very hilly in spots and best for strong bicyclists.

Google Map QR Code:

Orleans

The Rail Trail in Orleans travels through the countryside to Orleans Center and then north to Eastham. A side route to East Orleans brings you to the breathtaking vistas at Weeset, Nauset Beach, and Barley Neck.

Parking

Nickerson State Park: There is a large parking area to the right of the entrance building. Another lot is about 0.1 miles west on Route 6A, on the same side of the road as the Park entrance

Orleans Center: Park on Old Colony Way just off Main Street, in the small bike path parking there.

East Orleans: Parking for the East Orleans Route is at the town landing at Weeset, Barley Neck, or at Nauset Beach.

Trail Description — Rail Trail in Orleans

After passing through the underpass on Route 6A at Nickerson Park, the Trail passes several bogs and then a splendid view of Namskaket Creek to the left. After a short detour onto West Street to cross Route 6, the trail continues off-road over interesting terrain to Orleans Center. At Orleans center there are many stores, including a bike shop, restaurants, galleries, ice cream shops, and all services. From the center, you can continue directly on the Rail Trail to the bicycle bridge across Route 6. Just before Route 6 on the right are several fast food spots. At Main Street in Orleans, for many years, the rail trail went left to Rock Harbor. At Rock Harbor, there is a large parking area and a historical marker explaining the area's commercial importance in the late 1800's. The Harbor was the center of activity as packet boats arrived daily from Boston. Here also, the Battle of Rock Harbor took place, one of the only Cape battles with the British during the War of 1812.

Once over Route 6, the bike route proceeds to the right along the Creek to the large overhead power lines. Just past the courthouse, the arrow-straight off-road path continues through refreshing open countryside with fascinating views. Soon you will pass Boat Meadow; the smell of the marsh is pleasing, and the sea oats, marsh grass, and salt hay that was once used by the settlers as fodder provide for pleasant scenery. An alternate route to the north is Bridge Street (just to the left of the Courthouse) to Governor Prence Road and back to the trail. The distance is the same, but the views are exceptional, and there is access to the ocean along the way.

Trail Description — East Orleans

The suggested route begins at the landing in Tonset (see map) with its wonderful views of Coast Guard and Nauset

Beaches. It was in Nauset Harbor that Leif Ericson (1003), Gosnold and de Champlain (early 1600's) sailed. Here a telegraph cable from France came ashore beginning in the late 1890's. Tonset Road provides a pleasant ride with several long coasts. At Meeting House Road, turn sharp left and be sure to walk across the intersection at Hopkins Road. Turn left on Beach Road and at the Inn, turn right onto Barley Neck Road. After passing many views of the River to the left and some rolling terrain, you will come to a downhill stretch ending abruptly at a town landing. Here is a wonderful place to rest and

enjoy the views of Pochet Neck to the left and Pochet Island to the right.

From the landing, return uphill and turn right onto Twiss Road. There are several very sharp curves. From here you can see Nauset beach where the freighter Eldia grounded during a coastal storm in 1984. Continue, using the map, and keeping to the right to reach Cedar Land Road. Proceed up the hill. Explore the area, and don't miss Shore View Drive, Samoset Road and Old Duck Hill Road. Return to Cedar Land and take this right to Beach Road, which can be followed right to Nauset Beach, a town beach with full facilities, food, and large parking. Brick Hill Road (from Beach Street) will take you uphill mostly to the Tonset Road again.

Google Map QR Code:

F rom the Boat Meadow Marsh just north of the Orleans area, the bike path continues through the countryside to Locust Street, a scant half mile from the National Park Visitor Center at Salt Pond. A fine bike path to Coast Guard Beach, the Salt Pond Trail, also called the Nauset Trail, begins at the far end of the parking lot.

Parking

Salt Pond Visitor Center: From Route 6 in Eastham, park at the Salt Pond Center on the right.

Trail Description — Rail Trail in Eastham

From Boat Meadow, continue north on the ever-so-gentle

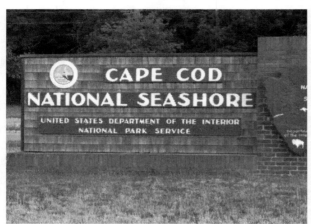 upslope to Governor Prence Road. Thomas Prence settled in the Eastham area in 1644, and was a influential land-owner and wealthy mer-chant. He was Governor of the Plymouth Colony several times from 1634 to 1672. Here, about 200 feet to the right on Governor Prence Road, see if you can spot the old cranberry bog. The bog is almost indistinguishable as such now, as it is filled with grasses, and small shrub due to the effects of the process of succession.

From Governor Prence Road, the rail trail edges up noticeably but gently, past several homes; it soon leaves the open to enter pitch pine stands just before Bridge Road. Then it is a short distance to a marvelous area with several beautiful views of Herring Pond to the left. Herring Pond is a kettle pond formed from a glacial ice block partially buried in the sand a the glacier retreated. About 43 acres in size, Herring Pond has a maximum depth of about 35 feet. Besides supporting trout, perch, and pickerel, the pond supports American alewife that annually swim upstream through the Herring Brook to the west of Herring Pond. A half-mile ride to the left on Crosby Village Road brings you to the herring run there and to views of the Herring River marshes.

To the right of the pond, just off the bike trail, it is only 25 yards through to the Bridge Road cemetery where a different, peaceful perspective of the pond can be had, and some fascinating old stones can be read. Continue now about 3/4 mile past sandy poverty-grass-covered hillsides and views of more kettle ponds to the left and the right. (Depot Pond). Soon you will pass a small stand of locusts and arrive, appropriately enough, at the locust-lined Locust Street. Here, though the rail trail continues north, bicyclists can turn right on Locust Road and then left on Salt Pond Road to get to Salt Pond Visitor Center. The center offers films, literature, advice, a free museum, restrooms and a bookstore. It is a very worthwhile stop with gorgeous views of Salt Pond just behind the Visitor Center and many fascinating displays about Cape Cod.

Trail Description — Salt Pond (Nauset) Trail

This three mile round trip takes you over land once inhabited by the Nauset native Americans and early settlers of Cape Cod. The Nausets were fishermen and farmers and grew corn, beans, squash, tobacco, and pumpkins on the hillsides here. At the far end of the parking lot, the path swings up to the right past some old apple trees, signs of the settlers' farming, past ivy-covered locusts and then through a large stand of locusts. A gentle coast downhill and then a steep uphill bring you to the cedar pine and oak-covered plain, once a golf course. The trail continues over the rolling countryside to a sitting bench, a fine place to rest and enjoy the scenery.

At the second stop sign and cross road, turn right off the bike trail to reach the Doane memorial. This is a monument to Deacon John Doane who built a home here in 1644. Imagine, if you can, living in this fine spot! Turning left off the trail brings you in 0.2 miles to Doane Rock Picnic area and the largest exposed glacial erratic boulder on Cape Cod. Returning to the bike path, keep your eyes open for views of the old Coast Guard Station framed by the trees and listen for sounds of the surf. You will soon reach the wooden bridge over the marsh; be sure to stop to enjoy the cool air and the splendid views and the sounds of nature.

From the bridge, it is a short ride up to the left to the station. The station is no longer a Coast Guard Station, and is now used by the National Park Service. Coast Guard Beach is a wonder in itself. Here several homes, a bath house, and a large parking area were destroyed by the blizzard of 1978, never to be replaced. The surf is high here, with twenty foot waves sometimes during a gale. Even Thoreau had noticed that the ocean was relentlessly cutting back the shore here. The spot is "huge and real", as he had noted. Swimming and walking, and as Henry Beston who lived here a year observing nature had noted, the "elemental things" are to be found and enjoyed at Coast Guard Beach, the Outermost Shore.

Google Map QR Code:

A s the Rail Trail continues directly north on very level terrain, the ever-narrower peninsula of Cape Cod brings the ocean views, sounds and breezes closer with every mile. The Great Island Route is 8 miles round trip along Mayo Beach and Chequesset Neck to Great Island where 4 miles of spectacular hiking trails are found.

Parking

South Wellfleet: The Rail Trail parking is at South Wellfleet, behind the general store, up on the hill, off of Lecount Hollow Road.

Wellfleet Center: For the Great Island route, proceed north on Route 6 past Eastham to the signs pointing to the left to

Wellfleet Center. Stay straight on Main Street to 300 Main Street, the Town Hall. There is a large parking area behind the Town Hall.

Great Island: Follow Chequessett Neck Road nearly to its end; there are two parking lots just at the sharp bend just before the end of the road. Additional parking is at the Town Pier and at Mayo Beach.

Trail Description — Rail Trail in Wellfleet

The trail continues north from Locust Road in Eastham along the power lines. Kingsbury Beach on the Cape Cod Bay, with tidal flats and soft sand, is 2 miles to the left on Kingsbury Road. The trail soon passes under Route 6 near a popular fast food restaurant; proceed slowly through the tunnel, as visibility is reduced somewhat due to the the curves. As you go north past Route 6, notice that the trees are stunted here from the ocean wind; this effect will become even more dramatic as you proceed farther north as the Cape becomes narrower and narrower and the ocean breezes grow stronger.

At Brackett Road there is ice cream, food and groceries and bicycle supplies 0.1 mile to the left. North from here, notice the many Atlantic white cedars and the low heath-type vegetation, both of which are tolerant of the ocean's nearly continuous salty breezes in this area and the dry sandy soil. At Nauset Road (then onto Railroad Avenue), a market deli and fast food are found; Nauset Beach with its famous lighthouse is 2 miles to the right on Nauset Road and is well worth a side trip; the scenery there is gorgeous.

As you continue north of Nauset Road on the Rail Trail, look for the stand of staghorn sumacs; it is said that natives used to use the berries as a lemonade drink. Past the boundary post marking Wellfleet's boundary you will pass over two dikes, the first one at Silver Spring Brook and the second, well worth a stop, at a beautiful small pond and wetland area – Fresh Brook. These both drain into Silver Spring Harbor on the bay side of Wellfleet; the area provides the spectacular location for the Wellfleet Audubon Sanctuary.

At the Marconi Beach Road crossing, Marconi Beach with its stunning views and surf is 1.7 miles to the right. This is the wild Atlantic of the outermost Cape at its best, expansive and overpowering; it is well worth a side trip. While recent erosion has liimited beach acess, you can still visit the Marconi Site itself (no swimming beach) which is reached by taking the Beach Road a few hundred feet to the right, then taking the Marconi Site Road on the left, following that road past the water tower, about a mile total. At the Marconi Site itself is a picnic area, fantastic views of the ocean, the White Cedar Swamp Trail (1 mile with boardwalks right along the Cedar Swamp) and of course, the site of the famous Marconi radio transmission. In

1903, Guglielmo Marconi had set up at this location the equipment needed to send the first wireless transmission from the United States, greetings from President Theodore Roosevelt to King Edward VII of England. This marked the beginning of radio transmissions as we know them today.

Back on the main Rail Trail, soon you will pass over the sometimes odorous Blackfish Creek area and reach Lecount Hollow Road; a fine general store is found here. It is just a mile here from west to east across Cape Cod. The Creek is named for the Blackfish, a species of whale that would often beach in this area at low tide. In the 1800's, part of Blackfish Creek was used as a harbor area for fishing and trading vessels, but late in the 1800's, all of the shipping activity moved to the main, deeper harbor in Wellfleet Center.

Presently the Cape Cod Rail Trail ends at Lecount Hollow Road. Future plans to extend the trail into Provincetown are being considered, but there are many difficulties with private property and the natural features in this area. Following Lecount Hollow Road 1 mile to the right from the Rail Trail will bring you to the dunes near Lecount Hollow Beach.

Trail Description — Great Island Route

The Great Island Route begins on Main Street in Wellfleet Center. There are several shops and restaurants in Wellfleet that make it a wonderful place to visit on its own. From the Town Hall parking area behind the Town Hall at 300 Main Street, turn left on Main Street and then turn right onto Whit's Lane. This brings you down to East Commercial Street. Just to the left, there is a pedestrian bridge to Cannon Hill, a short walk but an enjoyable one. This is "Uncle Tim's Bridge", recently restored by the Wellfleet Historical Commission. First built in 1783, the bridge spans Duck Creek. Timothy Daniels had operated a shop here in the 1800's, and was affectionately know as Uncle Tim, hence the name of the bridge. From the bridge itself you can see the mummichugs (minnows), clams, scallops, mussels; and breathe the refreshing marsh air. Take the pine woods path to the right up the Hill; you will end at a perfect place for a picnic, with extensive views of Wellfleet and the Point.

From the bridge access, continue biking west on East Com-

mercial Street, along the water and past several businesses, restaurants and classic New England homes to Wellfleet Town Pier where you will see commercial fishing and find cold snacks and wonderful views of Indian Head to the left and Great Island to the right. Just 1/4 mile farther there is a swimming area at Mayo Beach with parking and benches for resting.

Proceeding now along the shore, the road, now Kendrick Avenue, soon leads into Chequessett Neck Road. You can simply stay along the shore on this entire route. On Chequesset Neck road, the biking begins to rise steadily past marsh views, then past the Yacht Club, and to a high point where there is a clear view of the northeast-most part of Great Island and views back to Indian Neck and the coast of Eastham. Over the hill you will coast down to the bridge over Herring River. Notice the wind-stunted pines along here. Stop at the bridge to listen and to view – this is a charming spot. Well into the 1800's, Great Island was separated from the rest of Cape Cod here, it was truly an island, created by the glacier thousands of years ago.

The connection to the Cape, though, was caused by sand washing along the shore from Truro, connecting the islands of material that the glacier had left, and thus creating what is called a "tombolo", a sand connection of an island to the main land form. From here it is just a half mile farther on Chequessett Neck Road to the National Park area where there are picnic sites and a hiking trail that leads 4.1 miles to the end of Great Island – Jeremy Point. A shorter walk will bring you to the location of a tavern used by whaling captains during the 1700's, but there is no direct evidence of the tavern remaining at this time, just archeological evidence. The Great Island hike is a long walk, but a beautiful and inspiring one. A brochure and map is available here describing the geological and human history of the area.

Google Map QR Code:

Truro / Head of the Meadow

A pleasant trail of 4 miles round trip, this once was part of the "Old King's Highway" overland route to Provincetown. It provides views of the salt marsh and meadow in an area once exposed to the open sea; access to Pilgrim Spring, where the Pilgrims first found fresh water in the New World; and an access to the fine Head of the Meadow Beach.

Parking

High Head: Take Route 6 north past North Truro until Pilgrim Lake is just visible. Before reaching the lake, turn right onto High Head Road, just across Route 6 from the row of cottages. Follow this 1/4 mile, bearing left and not proceeding up the hill. Caution! This road is rough! A speed of 5 mph is recommended. The trail begins at the far end of the parking area on the right, not the left, which is the sand route.

Head of the Meadow: Take Beach Road from Route 6 to reach parking at Head of the Meadow Beach.

Trail Description – Head of the Meadow Trail

The High Head area that you saw to the right as you turned off Route 6 is one of the highest locations on Cape Cod. From the top of High Head, there are expansive views of Cape Cod Bay from Provincetown to the Canal. The Head of the Meadow Trail is a very level trail that passes through some unique ecological areas; it is an easy bike trail for children. At its beginning, there are views of the dunes to the left. The sand to form these dunes has for thousands of years been forced by wave action northward from Eastham and Truro and then moved inland by heavy winds each year. The hills to the right of the trail, including the High Head area, are moraines that were deposited by the glacier directly. The two terrains form a sharp contrast here, with the salt marsh between. Past the shrub-covered

hillsides, the trail continues along the marsh. Look for ferns, cattails, and also the typical saltmarsh plants. Notice the extensive ditching of the marsh for insect control.

Soon a small picnic area is found along the right of the trail. This is a quiet spot with dunes and marsh views. It was here, some claim, that the Pilgrims first found fresh water at Pilgrim Spring to the right. However, there is some room for question, and not everyone agrees that this was the spot; there are several possibilities in this area. The footpaths from the picnic area lead to another picnic area with direct access from Route 6, Pilgrim Heights.

Back on the bike path, the trail continues with only the slightest grades through interesting woods, mostly oak. Look for rabbits, as there are many in the area. Concentrate on the temperature change here as you bike; soon the ocean breeze will be distinctly felt as you move ever closer to the water. Can you also hear the surf as you bike?

The path eventually passes several pitch-pine-covered hills and comes close to the marsh again on the left. Continue to the Beach Road and turn left into the parking area to gain access to Head of the Meadow Beach. This would be a nice place to rest, swim, picnic, or walk. The views here are outstanding. The beach scarp here is quite high; the cliffs cannot exceed 34 degrees maximum slope here or the sand begins to slide, so the only beach access is on the stairways. This is a grand and special place. Certainly the eternal roar of the ocean, the grandeur of the sky, and the steep cliffs help us to put things in perspective here. Proceeding south from the parking area, a new bike trail will soon continue further south along the Old Kings Highway, through the woodlands to a small town beach.

Trail Description – North Truro Sideroute

This route is well worth the effort, as it takes you from one side of the Cape to the other, from the Atlantic shore to the Cape Cod Bay. Starting at the Highland Lighthouse area, you can see an extensive view of the open Atlantic, the foaming surf, and the incredible sky.

To the south is the former North Truro Air Force Radar facility, now operated by the Federal Aviation Administration and used to track trans-Atlantic flights into Boston and New York. During the Cold War, more than 500 personnel were stationed in North Truro. You can also see the famous Jenny Lind Tower, a fifty-five foot tower removed from Causeway Street in Boston's North End and rebuilt here as a memorial, supposedly, to Jenny Lind, a soporano who in the 1800's sang to Boston street crowds from its top. Unfortunately, because of its

proximity close to the radar facilities, the tower is not access-ible on foot at this time.

The Highland Lighthouse that you see here was built in 1857 to replace the first light built on the Cape, in 1798. The present structure was moved 490 feet back from the ocean in the 1990's due to extensive coastal erosion that threatened to topple the building. There is a fantastic observation platform behind the lighthouse, with views of the Atlantic that you will definitely remember. As you turn back from the platform, no-tice that you can see the ocean on the far side of Truro – clear across Cape Cod.

The bike route itself is interesting biking with some ocean views and a real glimpse of the quiet Truro countryside. Use extreme caution crossing Route 6A. In Truro there are several businesses, a small store, and several spots to eat. Chocolate, too! On the other side of Route 6A, you can see Pilgrim Pond on the left of Pond Street. A small memorial here commemor-ates the fact that the Pilgrims, on their second day here in

1690, had camped at this location. The Route soon follows Bay View Road to the left, and passes many fine homes with wonderful water views. Priest Road brings you to Hughes Road, and then back to Route 6A. Just to the right or left on Route 6A, depending on which road you take from Priest Road, is Truro Vineyards where you can see the vineyards right from the road or the parking area. The Route continues back to Highland Light by returning to Highland Road.

Google Map QR Code:

T hese five trails, about seven miles in length, pass over the undulating dunes of the Provincelands area and over successions of sand spits, each one built north of its predecessor to form the Provincetown area. From protected, shallow ponds to dunes covered with wind-gnarled trees, from stunning views of the Massachusetts mainland to beautiful beaches, these trails, though hilly, offer much to the cyclist.

Parking

Beech Forest Parking: Take Route 6 north 2.3 miles past Pilgrim Lake on the Truro/Provincetown line, turning right onto Race Point Road. Access to the trail is available at the large Beech Forest Parking Area 0.3 miles on the left.

Provincelands Visitor Center: Continue on Race Point Road past the Beech Forest Parking area to the Visitor Center on the right.

Herring Cove Beach: Take Route 6 north to its end at Route 6A, turning left on Route 6A to reach Herring Cove Beach parking area on the right.

Trail Description —

Loop Trail from Beech Forest to Visitor Center

After leaving the Beech Forest Parking Area, cross the Race Point Road onto the bike path which will take you over rolling terrain through a pitch-pine-covered sand dune area, and then past a small pond on the right. As you bike, notice the many dead pitch pines, killed by burial in constantly moving sands, and note the many dying trees as well. This is a difficult environment for plants, with very sandy soil and heavy winds. The trail continues up from here, following the Race Point Road through oak woods with dunes to the right, and then the bike path veers off through the woods.

At the Provincelands Visitor Center to the left of the trail, information about the biology, geology, and history of the area is available. From the observation platforms you can see exceptional views of Race Point Beach, the old Coast Guard Station, and the surrounding areas. The Coast Guard Station is now on Commercial Street in Provincetown, closer to the main Provincetown Harbor. The large white, old Coast Guard Station building that you see at Race Point had been built there in 1931 and operated as the Coast Guard Station until 1979. The building is now used by the National Park Service. The mainland of Massachusetts can at times also be seen from the upper observation platform of the Visitor Center, and whales may be spotted if conditions are right. The Center is staffed by a naturalist, and offers a bike rack, restroom facilities, drinking water, descriptive displays, and parking.

Visitor Center to Race Point Beach

From the Visitor Center, this trail section brings you by downhill coasting over pitch-pine-covered dunes. Look for the

many lichens and Scotch Broom that can survive in these harsh conditions. Continuing uphill, the trail crosses Race Point Road, and then goes right toward the Provincetown Airport. The trail continues, primarily uphill, to the parking area at the Race Point Beach, where there are full restroom and beach facilities in season. It was near Race Point Beach that the famous playwright Eugene O'Neill lived and wrote in a shack for some time. The shack, unfortunately, was a victim of shore erosion in 1931. The rough seas in this area have taken many ships over the years as well. It is not uncommon to see whales offshore in this area.

From Race Point Paralleling Provincelands Road

This section heads left after crossing Race Point Road, heading toward the Herring Cove Beach area. The trail heads sharply to the right at first, up a steep hill and then down a long, fine coast over the dunes, all the while offering splendid views. Look for the beachgrass that stabilizes the area by restricting sand motion, and for the poverty grass. The trail continues under the Provincelands Road, then follows on its left, with views of the dunes area, Provincetown center, and Pilgrim Monument to the left over the dunes. The monument was built of Maine granite in 1907-1910 and cost $95,000. It was built to commemorate the Pilgrims who landed in Provincetown before they headed for quieter harbors at Plymouth where they ultimately began the Plymouth settlement. Over 252 feet high on a 100 foot hill, the monument and museum there provide views of all of the surrounding areas and even as far as Boston on a clear day; it is a wonderful place to visit itself.

Provincelands Road to Beech Forest Trail

This section returns over hilly terrain and through marsh and woods past numerous fine pond views and marsh views to the Beech Forest Trail and parking area. Be sure to take the short Bennett Pond trail along the way to view the beautiful ponds there.

Provincelands Road to Herring Cove Beach

This trail is a winding path that skirts the Snake Hills, steep and closely situated hillsides. The trail continues to the fine and popular Herring Cove Beach, where everyone can enjoy this breezy location. Parking is also available for many cars. In recent years, though, considerable erosion of the parking lot area itself has been a problem for the Park Service in maintaining access to the area as much as there had been in the past. Work in 2023 will create a Route 6 Bike Trail Connector that will parallel the terminal 800 feet of Route 6; additional work is planned to eventually make a trail along Route 6 all the way to Shank Painter Road.

Google Map QR Code:

One of the most pleasant routes on Cape Cod, this well-planned bike route visits breathtaking sights of Stage Harbor, Chatham Bars, Chatham Lighthouse, Chatham Coast Guard Station, and the Chatham Fish Pier. The route is about 8 miles long, with many places to stop. It is a fine ride for a bright summer day. Don't forget to visit Chatham's renowned Main Street shops after your ride.

Parking

Chatham Fish Pier: Take Route 28 to the Chatham Rotary, and at the rotary, continue toward North Chatham on Route 28. Follow this to Barcliff Road, then turn right on Barcliff, taking this to Shore Road. Just to the right on Shore Road is the Fish Pier area, on the left of the road.

Oyster Pond: Take Route 28 to the Chatham Rotary, then turn right onto Stage Harbor Road. Follow this to the Oyster Pond parking area on the right.

Trail Description – Chatham Bike Route

At the Chatham Fish Pier you can see commercial fishing activities and also buy fresh fish or lobster. Ample parking and facilities are available. This is a fine place to explore before or after your bike ride and to get the flavor of Cape Cod's fishing industry. Be sure to check out the fantastic views from the elevated viewing platform behind the main building. The bike route itself begins by heading right along Shore Road and uphill toward the lights. Turn here to the right, following Old Harbor Road down the steep hill. The views here are gorgeous.

Turn right at the end of the road and follow Scatteree Road to its end to Scatteree Landing at Allen Point. At Scatteree Landing, there is a splendid view to the right of Nauset Beach, the barrier beach which extends south from Orleans, and which was breached by a storm in 2007; Strong Island is to the left. The barrier beach is a continually moving and tenous protection to the mainland here.

Continue the bike route by going back up from the landing, and past the Salt Pond on your left and up the hill. This will lead you onto Stoney Hill Road and then across Route 28 at the gas station. Proceeding on Stoney Hill Road and down the hill there, use caution as you turn left onto Lake Street and then onto Crowell Road. At Route 28. the route passes food stores, restaurants, gasoline stations, and outdoor soda machines.

Across the highway, the route passes to the left of the inn and then down to the parking area just to the left of Oyster Pond. Here there is a fine vista with Chatham "Neck" on the left, West Chatham on the right. The bike route continues at the far side of the small beach area. Uphill and right onto Cedar Street, the route passes an area of fine homes and then begins a long coast downhill to lowlands with scrub pine, brush, and scrub oak. At the end of Cedar Street, turn left on Battlefield Road and then right onto Sears Road. Stay on Sears Road to its end and you will reach a narrow town landing with a wonderful view of Stage Harbor, Hardings Beach, the picturesque lighthouse and the entrance of Stage Harbor to the left. Built in 1880, the cast iron lighthouse operated until 1933 when it was replaced by a navigation tower. Presently, the building is a private residence. Return up Sears Road to Battlefield Road. The bike route, though, continues on Champlain Road, and up the hill on that twisting road. At the sharp left turn, there are views to the right of Stage Harbor and Morris Island. Continuing, you will reach Old Mill Boat Yard and Chatham Fisheries area, great places to get the flavor of boating and fishing on Cape Cod.

From there, turn left and then at the stop sign, right onto Bridge Street. Here proceed downhill to the Mitchell River, crossing near the Monomoy Yacht Club, with Mill Pond on the left. This was for many years a wooden drawbridge, but had become structurally deficient and was in need of reconstruction. After considerable controversy about using metal or wood to replace the historic structure, it was decided to maintain the historic appearance of the bridge as much as possible. Passing over the bridge, proceed on Bridge Street, but use especial caution in this area as drivers may be sightseeing. Continue to the sharp, dangerous, twisting turn to the left which brings you to the Chatham Light area.

Here at the Chatham Light area, there is a magnificent view of the inlet, the tidal flats, and the far reaches of Nauset Beach. Several winter storms have severed the Nauset peninsula at this location. First built as twin lights in 1808, and using lard oil as fuel, the lighthouse itself was replaced in 1841 and again in 1877 as the shore eroded back. Seen 25 miles to sea, its 2,800,000 candlepower light is a lifesaver and important for navigation in the area.

From the Chatham Light area, a side route to Tom's Neck and Morris Island will bring you breathtaking views and end at the National Oceanic and Atmospheric Administration's weather facility at Chatham and the headquarters for the Monomoy National Wildlife Refuge, where informational displays, hiking trails, and stunning views are available. The area has recently been in the news for the large seal population and the great white sharks that frequent the area as a result. It is a little tricky to find the headquarters, but well worthwhile: just continue about a hundred yards past the private area signs, a bit up the hill, and then turn left to enter the headquarters area.

The main route continues north from Chatham Light uphill past fine views, passing Chatham Bars Inn on the left, and eventually bringing you back to the Chatham Fish Pier area.

Trail Description – Old Colony Rail Trail – Chatham

The Old Colony Rail Trail in Chatham begins in Harwich as a spur off of the Cape Cod Rail Trail which itself continues north toward Brewster from the Harwich area.

On the Old Colony Trail, just past Route 137, there is a nice ice cream stop on the right. The bike trail itself continues past the Chatham landfill to Sam Ryder Road and then to George

Ryder Road. At George Ryder Road 0.2 miles to the right is Route 28, with many restaurants from fast foods to sit down. The trail then passes Chatham airport where sightseeing plane rides are available, and then passes beautiful White Pond on the right. With some of the trail following and crossing paved roads in spots, we soon arrive at Crowell Road.

Here, you can connect to the Chatham route above, or can go to the right directly into Chatham center to visit this classic Cape Cod village.

Google Map QR Code:

Please Bicycle Carefully During Your Visit!

It's the law in Massachusetts: children must wear
protective helmets when bicycling.
And adults should wear helmets, too!

During your visit, for your own safety and health:

1. Don't bicycle on dangerous routes — stay on easy off-road paths. If the traffic is heavy, bike that route at a later date.
2. Be sure to *walk* across all road crossings, even on the Rail Trail, and don't let children bike too far ahead of you.
3. Obey all motor traffic laws and signs; especially, be sure to use hand signals.
4. Keep to the right on bike paths, bike in single file, and don't speed. Always pass on the left and give warning when passing.
5. Don't even think of drinking or texting and bicycling!
6. Check your bicycle before bicycling — tires, brakes, and reflectors.
7. Watch out for splinters on the railings along the trail. Don't use your hands to stop!
8. Watch out for objects on the path — rocks, glass, drainage grates in the wrong positions.
9. Remember that poison ivy is common on the Cape.
10. Don't forget that ticks are virtually everywhere on Cape Cod and they can carry serious diseases.
11. Don't bicycle with pets! They can frighten children and cause accidents.
12. Bring suntan lotion or a suncreen. You'll bike better if

you're not so red!

13. Lock your car, don't carry valuables in it, and don't leave bikes unattended.

14. Keep yourself visible! Don't bike at night and always wear bright clothing.

15. Please don't litter. Cape Cod is very clean! Please help to keep it that way!

Cape Cod Weather

Keep an eye on the sky and listen to weather forecasts when you visit Cape Cod. The weather is very changeable and winds and rain can be intense.

Cape Cod often offers ideal bicycling conditions, but it is not immune to poor weather.

Average daily high temperature in May is 62, in June 71, in July 78, in August 76, and in September 70.

September and October are especially fine months for bicycling on the Cape, but the Cape's warm winters and cool summers invite the bicyclist year round.

National Weather Service
7 Day Forecast for Cape Cod:

About the Cape Cod Rail Trail

The Cape Cod Rail Trail was built along the right of way of the Pennsylvania Central Railroad. Built in the early 1880's by the Old Colony Railroad Compnay to meet the demands of an expanding tourist trade, the railroad was used most heavily by visitors from New York and Boston. The line later became the New York, New Haven and Harford Railroad, and then Pennsylvania Central Railroad.

With the Canal bridges built in the 1930's, and the use of trucks and automobiles increasing, the railroad lost favor and was eventually abandoned in 1965. In 1978, the Department of Environmental Management purchased the right of way of the Railroad, and began to design the trail for use by bicyclists and pedestrians.

Construction from Dennis to Eastham was completed in 1983 and from Eastham north to South Wellfleet in 1994. Route 6 overpasses in Brewster and in Orleans were added in 2002-3 and the extension to Chatham in 2004; reconstruction of the entire trail was done in 2006 and 2007. An extension from Dennis to West Yarmouth in 2018 with a new bridge over Bass River connected the Yarmouth Trail to the rest of the Cape Cod Rail Trail, making the Rail Trail start in Yarmouth.

The resulting trail is a unique and special attraction on Cape Cod, and we hope that you enjoy its use.

About the Author

William E. Peace holds both Bachelor's and Master's degrees from Tufts University and has taught science on Cape Cod since 1973 at both the secondary and undergraduate levels. An avid nature enthusiast and bicyclist, he has lived on Cape Cod for over forty years and knows the area as only a local resident could. He has also led walks at Sandy Neck Barrier Beach, and worked as a research associate at the Cape Cod National Seashore.

The author of several books and webpages, Bill has three grown children. Besides his family, Bill is interested in photography, camping and the outdoors, computers and education, and gardening.

Bill's books include *The Cape Cod Bike Book* which was first published in 1984 and is still the go-to guide on Cape bicycling, authored by a local Cape Cod resident, and published and revised annually. He also has published a new series of *Cape Cod Visitor's Guides: Free and Inexpensive Things to Do* on the Cape, with books about the Upper Cape, Mid Cape, Lower Cape, and Outer Cape.

Each book gives a real insider's view to the Cape, information about points of interest, notes on history, ecology, where to stop, what to see, and some things that you might otherwise miss along the way. Bill loves Cape Cod, and he wants you to love it too, and he shares that passion in all the work that he does.

For more information about things to see on Cape Cod, check out Bill's main webpage, at *williampeacecapecod.com* The page has links to his other pages about bicycling on the Cape, lighthouses on Cape Cod, windmills on Cape Cod, walks and hikes on Cape Cod, playgrounds on Cape Cod, and things to do on rainy days on Cape Cod.

About QR Codes

QR stands for Quick Response. QR codes are similar to bar codes and were first used in 1994 in automobile manufacturing to keep track of parts for the vehicle. Now, they are used extensively for many purposes, including providing quick access to web pages.

In our book, each QR code brings you to a custom Google Map which will show you the exact location of the trail that you are looking for, as well as the other roads in the area, and where to park. The only information in the QR code is the web address of the map, nothing else; there is no tracking at all of the use of the code. The QR code simply saves having to type in a lengthy address to find the map.

You can just use your cell phone to view the QR code, and then the map will be opened quickly and easily on your phone. Once the map opens, you can zoom in to see the trail and area roads in detail; you can switch from street map view to satellite view and zoom in on the location. And, as you bike, you will always have the map with you, right on your phone.

If you click on a star in the map view, it will use the star as your destination and you can then use Google Maps to guide you automatically that trail location using your cell phone as a free GPS. This is amazing technology, linking the printed book with our cellphones! If you prefer, our book also has detailed written directions for each location as well, including exactly how to get to each spot in the book and where to park.

Many phones now have QR code reading already built in to the camera. If your phone does not have a QR code reader already installed, you can find many apps that will read QR codes either in the Google Store or on Apple; just search for "QR Code." You also need to have the Google Maps app installed, as well as the Chrome app. Your location must be allowed in the app permission settings for both Chrome and Google maps.

PHOTOGRAPHS

Cape Cod Canal

Sagamore Bridge (p. 5), Mainland Side of Canal (p. 6), Sagamore Bridge (p. 8), Packed and Parked (p. 9), Sagamore Bridge (p. 10), Cape Cod Canal (p. 11), Near Herring Run (p. 12)

Falmouth Shining Sea Trail

Quisset Beach (p. 14), Nobska Road (p. 15), Woods Hole (p. 16), Nobska Light (p. 17), Chapaquoit Beach (p. 18)

Osterville/Marstons Mill/Mashpee

Oyster Harbors Windmill (p. 20), Crosby Boat Yard (p. 21), Bridge Street Town Landing (p. 22), Dead Neck Island (p. 23), Osterville Center (p. 24)

Lewis Bay, Hyannisport

Hyannis Harbor (p. 26), Bay Shore Road Landing (p. 27), Lewis Bay (p. 28), Nantucket Ferry from Kennedy Memorial (p. 29), Kennedy Memorial (p. 30)

Yarmouth

Yarmouth Bike Path (p. 32), Pedestrian Bridge Station Av-

Wellfleet

Marconi Beach (p. 66), Marconi Site (p. 68), South Well-fleet General Store (p. 69), Wellfleet Town Hall (p. 70), View from Tim's Bridge (p. 71), Great Island (p. 72)

Truro

Head of the Meadow Beach (p. 73), Dunes at Head of Meadow (p. 74), Highland Lighthouse (p. 76), Federal Aviation Radar and Jenny Lind Tower (p. 77), Pilgrim Pond (p. 78)

Provincelands

Provincetown from MacMillan Pier (p. 79), MacMillan Pier (p. 80), Provinclands Visitor Center (p. 81), Race Point Trail (p. 82), Provincelands Road Trail (p. 83), Old Coast Guard Station (p. 84)

Chatham

Chatham Lighthouse (p. 85), Fishing Boat in Chatham (p. 86), Mitchell River (p. 87), Old Mitchell River Drawbridge (p. 88), Monomoy Island (p. 89), Chatham Light Beach (p. 90)

Cape Cod Bicycle Trails and Routes

Made in United States
Troutdale, OR
01/22/2024

17069766R00060